D1134563

THE MILLS & BOON®
MODERN GIRL'S GUIDE TO
Helping Yourself

HQ
An imprint of HarperCollinsPublishers Ltd.
1 London Bridge Street
London SE1 9GF

This hardback edition 2016

1

First published in Great Britain by
HQ, an imprint of HarperCollinsPublishers Ltd. 2016

A catalogue record for this book is
available from the British Library

ISBN: 978-0-00-821235-3

Printed and bound in Italy

Funny, feisty and feminist:
The Mills & Boon Modern Girl's Survival Guides.

Introduction

Another sunrise, another day spent pondering your own internal weather, with overcast skies, monsoons and metaphorical wheelie bins merrily blowing down the streets of your mind. Life is hard - terrible love interests, woeful work colleagues, no Wi-Fi when you need it. And that's before you get to your own deep-seated character flaws.

Other hippy-happy self-help books will encourage you to 'turn that frown upside down', which is all well and good if you're a slightly sad sunbeam who has temporarily lost sight of the rainbow, but more tricky if you're stuck in a blizzard of procrastination, with a hailstone for a heart. You need something more cyclonic to pitch you out of the fog of self-doubt. Thankfully, help is at hand in this invaluable guide to self-improvement.

Don't despair: the barometer may be set to far from fair, but there are any number of solutions to the inescapable problem of You. Small steps make for big changes and once you've upgraded your expectations, learnt to love your inner child, embarked on an extensive, intensive course of crystal therapy, mindfulness, past life regression, yoga, detoxing and Hygge, you can turn into the person you've always dreamed of being. Or at least learn to stop slouching quite so much.

Affirmations

You are the architect of your own life

You are valuable, like a jewel or a set
of Beanie Babies

You are a divine river of compassion

Except for when it comes to Jean, you
don't have compassion for Jean

Not after she 'forgot' to invite
you to her baby shower

You are graceful like a swan or an expensive horse

Blogging

Reasons My Lifestyle Blog Is Significantly Less
Popular Than Gwyneth Paltrow's 'Goop':

My lack of celebrity

My near-daily inability to remember my login details

My solution to every life problem being
'Eat a Massive Bowl of Doughnuts'

YOU DON'T HAVE TO DO THIS
When You take
the
NU-
SYSTEM
MEMORY COURSE

Brain Training

Thanks to the Nu-System Memory Course,
Matilda can now remember every single social
faux-pas she has ever committed with
crystal-clear, fist-biting clarity.

Conscious Uncoupling

Sure, there were kinder ways of letting
Darren know that it was over.

But Chantelle always enjoyed a nautical theme,
and the moment just seemed *right*.

Cosmic Ordering

Dear Universe,

Someone told me that you're like an infinitely expanding Santa, and that if I ask you for stuff I'll get it - so I would like:

A massive bowl of doughnuts
Abdominal muscles
A dog that does household chores for me

Ideally I would like the dog to respond to the name 'Chips', but this is not a deal-breaker.

Yours in anticipation,
Ada

De-cluttering

Now that she was camped out in the back garden, wearing the bathroom rug as a frock, Clara had the distinct feeling that she might have taken the whole de-cluttering mantra way too far.

Exercise

Fads Jules has Tried, None of Which
Have Lasted More Than a Week:

Prancercise!

Rock Hard Thighs the Mexican Way

Five Second Glutes

Staring Hard at the Exercise Bike
You Use As a Drying Rack

Emaciated Doll Boxing

Exfoliate

'. . . Yeah, it's my own recipe. Mostly cheese and guacamole. Doesn't do much for the pores but goes really well with Pringles.'

Finding Yourself

This exotic world trip is where Olivia hopes
to finally find herself.

She has been planning it for three years.

She's pinned this giant map to the wall, stocked up
on malaria tablets, read *Eat Pray Love*, and bought
two dozen miniature travel shampoos.

Olivia will never quite get round to going any further
than the M25, but that's ok because, as it turns
out, she finds herself with a nice plumber
from Croydon.

Flossing

Things That Will Happen Before Naomi
Adopts a Regular Flossing Routine:

The accumulation of enough unopened dental
floss to stretch to Aberdeen and back

Britney's fifth comeback

Heat death of the universe

Guru

It was at the point that he started banging on
about the importance of 'everyone getting naked'
in order to 'be more in tune with our animal selves'
that Mollie started to think it might be time
to find a new guru.

Hygge

June couldn't be bothered to look up the exact definition, but she knew it was a Danish lifestyle thing, so she figured that just meant bacon, and lots of it.

Intelligent Budgeting

Rent - £750

Gas and Electricity - £60

TV Licence - £12

Betting on Illegal Backyard Duck Races - £8,900

Broadband - £24

Council Tax - £65

Now that she'd written down her monthly outgoings, it was pretty obvious to Kate that there was no way she could justify the amount she was spending on broadband.

January Detox

After four weeks of nothing but grapefruits,
Jill will discover that 'detoxing' is a myth, and
realise that if she'd bothered listening in GCSE
biology she'd have known our kidneys automatically
do the job of removing harmful toxins – that being
the whole point of kidneys.

Hanger and vengeance are a heady mix.

Kick-Starter

She'd hit her funding target in a week, but - never a whizz at financial matters - Mary had quite badly bungled the exchange rate, so her start-up selling fancy artisanal pizzas for 25 cents each would turn out to be a disaster.

Life-Hacks

Francine's Life Hacks:

Tie a ribbon to your suitcase to spot
it instantly at baggage reclaim

Add a teaspoon of baking soda to the water when
boiling an egg to make the shell easier to peel off

Pretend you have a romantic disease like
consumption to make people bring you tea

Makeover

It *is* what you asked for.
It's the 'Rachel'. From the *Friends* show.

I don't watch a lot of TV, but *Friends* was definitely the one about the monk solving crimes in medieval times.

I'm 100 per cent certain I've got that right.

Making the Best of Things

Today will be different.
Today will be different.
Today will be different.

Today wasn't different.

New Age Therapies

Posy's Definitive Guide to Crystal Healing:

Jade - strengthens bones, good for eyesight

Onyx - helps calm nervous disorders

Obsidian - helps settle the stomach after eating an entire Viennetta in one sitting

Ruby - attracts moths and unsuitable guys with motorbikes

Pearl - will make Colin text you

Emerald - improves skin, teeth, eyebrows

New Squad Goals

Janine has decided to replace her old social circle with a fun new social circle who won't be so negative all the time.

A social circle who won't judge her or make comments like:

'Janine, it's weird to make "friends" out of dolls,'

Or 'Janine, it's even weirder to cut pictures of movie stars' faces out of a magazine which you then stick to their heads.'

Overcoming Phobias

Maybe exposure therapy wasn't the
best way for Faye to deal with her
killer ape phobia after all.

Positive Thinking

Bella is attempting to go to her Happy Place.

Unfortunately, her Happy Place is located a little way past her Justified Fears About Her Relationship Place, across from her Overpowering Career Anxiety Place and right next door to her General Thoughts About the State of the World Place.

Posture

Michelle is feeling mighty pleased with her clever short cut to the old balance-a-book-on-your-head-for-perfect-posture diktat.

She'll be less happy when she realises she's used the wrong glue, and will have to spend the next six months with a copy of *Don't Sweat the Small Stuff* and *Seven Habits of Highly Effective People* stuck to her head.

Preparation

Frieda had made sure she was ready for bird flu, pig flu, zombie plague, meteor strike, and nuclear Armageddon.

Then it ended up being the bloody ice caps melting, the one thing she'd left off the list.

Typical.

Procrastination

Genevieve is well aware that procrastination
is the archenemy of productivity.

Which is why, right before she gets round to
cleaning the flat, she is making a shadow rabbit
super hero to kick procrastination's
task-avoiding ass.

Quitting

Having tried vaping, patches, gum and hypnotherapy,
Paula was embracing the patented 'puppet method'
– where you enjoy cigarettes vicariously via your
puppet chain-smoking all day.

Figure 1:

Figure 2:

Random Acts of Kindness

Figure 1: The type of 'good deed' I picture myself doing (elaborate costumes; a beached ship; maybe a doomed romantic couple).

Figure 2: The type of 'good deed' I have actually done (created matching hats for me and Providence, next door's totally under accessorized dog).

Reading

This year Amelia is determined to better herself by skim-reading the Wikipedia summaries of at least ten Booker-prize-winning novels.

After she is done with that she hopes to pass off some of the shorter reviews she can find on Goodreads as her own opinion at dinner parties.

Recharging
Your Batteries

Breakdown of Estelle's 'Working From Home' Day:

Alarm, two star jumps

Post-breakfast snooze

Nap

Pre-lunch forty winks

Post-lunch power nap

Mid-afternoon slump

Brief pre-EastEnders rest-time

Falling asleep on the dog

Bed

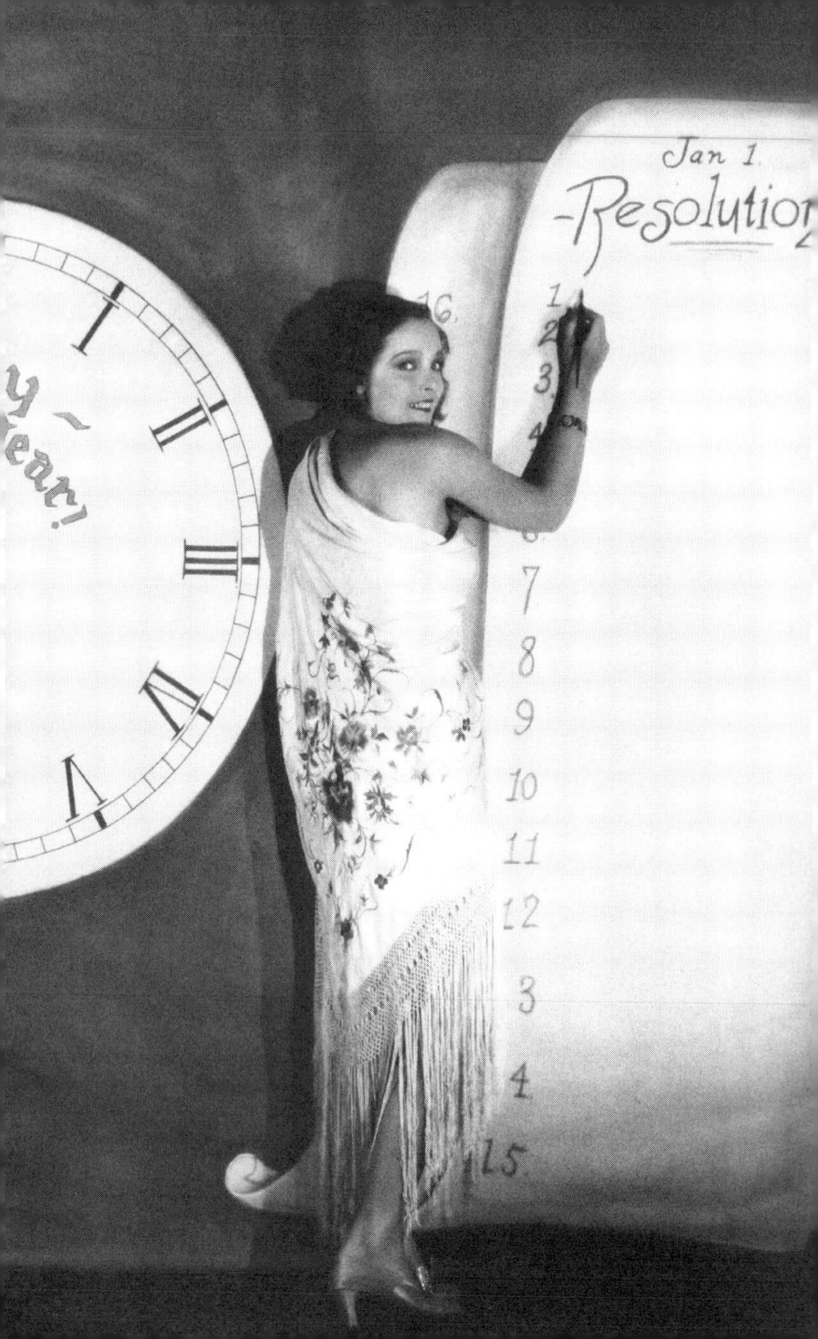
Jan 1.
-Resolution
1
2
3.
4
7
8
9
10
11
12
3
4
15.
16.

Resolutions

Emily's 2017 Resolutions

Go swimming at least once a week

Learn French

Crush the humans

Take up piano

Get up earlier

Stop saying 'crush the humans'
in case it gives the game away

Sort out finances

Ensure the device is fully operational

Eat more kale

Self-Help Seminar

At £600 for the weekend, plus accommodation,
Louise had assumed the 'Overcoming Life Hurdles'
course would be a bit more, you know,
metaphorical than this.

Start an Allotment

It seems like a good way to get back in touch with nature, and it's all breezy larks and sisterhood now, but in five months' time at the county's Biggest Marrow competition this will be a bloodbath.

Taking It Back

There were probably more pressing issues when it came to sisters doing it for themselves, but Phyllis had decided 'Man-Spreading On Public Transport' was going to be the fun thing she reclaimed from a male dominated world this week.

Treat Yo'self

Ways to Pamper Yourself:

Stick a load of sparklers in your hat

Wear much less flammable clothing

Practise the 'stop, drop and roll'
fire prevention technique

Have less stupid pampering ideas in the future

Unplugging

If you take apart all of Viv's electronic devices
and lay the components end to end, you'll have
a really arty Instagram post.

Very Bad Motivational Posters

That High-Budget Sci-Fi Movie Did Great At The Box Office And It Was Terrible, Like You

Don't Tell Me The Sky's The Limit When There Are Footprints On The Moon Set That NASA Definitely Faked

You Will Probably Lose Your Deposit By Sticking This 'Hang On In There' Poster Up, Your Landlord Specified That In Your Lease

Writer's Block

Don't know what Dorothy's smiling about, five months and she's just typed the word 'bums' over and over again.

X-Factor

Molly has decided to give up her high-powered, six-figure-salary City job in order to pursue her dream of becoming a star in the world of interpretive dance.

Her friends all say that it's a really great idea.

Molly's friends are bad friends.

Yoga

Marge's Top Three Ways to Achieve Inner Serenity:

3. The downward dog.

2. Greeting the sun.

1. A packet of Jaffa Cakes and half a bottle of Cava.

You Only Live Once

Anna is going to definitively prove this when her misguided, self-funded balloon flight doesn't quite go to plan.

Zen

Signs Your Chakras Might Be Off-Kilter:

Feelings of insecurity

Loss of will-power

Clinging onto the back of the train for dear life.

About Ada Adverse

Throughout her youth Ada joined several popular cults, undertook spiritual quests, and even appeared in an episode of The Crystal Maze. In 2006, after a conscious uncoupling from her family for tax reasons, she set up a popular lifestyle and mindfulness blog where she promotes her unique pine-cone based gut exfoliation diet, which has now been banned by the US food and drug administration and labelled 'hazardous and irresponsible' by the world health organisation. Her agony aunt column in Angling Times has been popular for years.

About Mills & Boon®

Since 1908, Mills & Boon® have been a girl's best friend.

We've seen a lot change in the years since: enjoying sex as a woman is now not only officially fine but actively encouraged, dry shampoo has revolutionised our lives and, best of all, we've come full circle on gin.

.

But being a woman still has its challenges. We're under-paid, exhaustingly objectified, and under-represented at top tables. We work for free from 19th November, and our life-choices are scrutinised and forever found lacking. Plus: PMS; unsolicited d*ck pics; the price of tights.

Sometimes, a girl just needs a break.
And, for a century, that's where we've come in.

So, to celebrate one hundred years of wisdom (or at least a lot of fun), we've produced these handy A-Zs: funny, feisty, feminist guides to help the modern girl get through the day.

We can't promise an end to the bullsh*t.
But we can offer some light relief along the way.